AF375557

JUGGLING ROMANCE AND PARENTHOOD

How to balance your family and your love life

Written by Aurélie Dorchy
In collaboration with Antonella Delli Gatti
Translated by Emma Hanna

Health and Wellbeing | 50MINUTES.com

When is it appropriate to leave parental responsibilities temporarily aside?

What can we do to forestall criticism from those around us regarding our parenting methods?

How can we juggle our professional, family and romantic lives simultaneously?

How can I make my partner realise that they are spending too much time with the children?

- What aspects of becoming a parent can threaten a romantic relationship?
- What specific steps can we take to get our children to respect our need for privacy?
- When is it appropriate to leave parental responsibilities temporarily aside?
- What can we do to forestall criticism from those around us regarding our parenting methods?
- How can we juggle our professional, family and romantic lives simultaneously?
- How can I make my partner realise that they are spending too much time with the children?

Modern couples tend to have fewer children than in bygone eras. This means that nowadays, children are cherished even more because they are rarer, and because their parents truly chose to have them. However, society is constantly putting more pressure on all of us to be increasingly successful, which can lead to a desire to be perfect in the eyes of our children.

Before you know it, they will start making an increasing number of untimely requests of you,

JUGGLING ROMANCE AND PARENTHOOD

HOW TO BALANCE YOUR FAMILY AND YOUR LOVE LIFE

- **Problem:** when you are used to sharing precious, intimate moments with your partner, you may fear that having children will jeopardise that aspect of your relationship. If you already have children, you may be letting your responsibilities towards them overwhelm you. Devoting yourself to them while also nurturing your relationship can be a difficult balancing act.
- **Aim:** to maintain (or even strengthen) your romantic relationship while also taking on all the responsibilities of being a parent.
- **FAQs:**
  - Our child does not want to let us have any time to ourselves. What should we do?
  - Should we be thinking about having a second child even if we had difficulty adjusting when we had our first child?

and you will end up spending more time playing your role as a parent than acting as an independent individual or taking precious moments to nurture your romantic relationship. But is it really possible to pour your heart and soul into living for your children, never taking any time to indulge in your own passions or to make the most of your relationship with your partner, without feeling like something is missing?

Of course, spending time with your children is fundamentally important, but you are still two adults who are in a romantic relationship, and you will need to spend time acting as adults. There is no obligation to spend all of your time talking about babies, school and "the little terror".

This short guide will show you how to gradually take back some of your time for yourself and your partner without neglecting your children's upbringing or the quality time you spend with them. On the contrary, this will make the time you spend with your children more meaningful, because it will no longer represent an obstacle to your romantic relationship or prevent you from recharging your batteries.

WHAT HAPPENS WHEN YOU LET THE ROMANCE DIE?

DECIDING TO HAVE CHILDREN TOGETHER

Every couple is different. Each of the individuals involved has their own life story, their own personality, and their own goals. Furthermore, everyone has different opinions about how to raise a child. All couples need to be constantly working on a shared vision for their family life, and a child's place in their life will be determined by the motivations behind and the strength of their desire to have children. Several different examples are outlined below:

- Both partners want to have a child, perhaps because they want to start a new chapter in their lives, or to give their relationship or their marriage a deeper meaning, because they want the chance to pass their own values on to their offspring, or perhaps even because they are consciously or unconsciously seeking to fill a hole in their lives.

- One partner is less certain about having a child than the other, or may even be entirely opposed to the idea. However, there are many people who agree to have a child, despite their underlying uncertainty, in order to please their partner or because they are afraid of disappointing them. In some cases, couples may split up if one of the people involved has personal reasons for not wanting children, enabling each of them to live their own lives.
- One partner desperately wants a child because they think that this will fill a hole in their life. This can lead them to become disproportionately invested in their child's upbringing.

Ideally, both partners should feel completely ready to have a child and to take on all of the responsibilities that come with that choice, or they may become frustrated and regret putting their own hopes and plans aside.

<u>TEST YOURSELF</u>

The following test may seem somewhat simplistic, but it can be revealing. Asking your partner the questions below will give you an idea of how they envision the role of being a parent and help you to identify their possible fears. This tool can help you to open a more constructive dialogue with them, and to prepare more effectively for having a child – or to realise that you are not as ready to have one as you had previously thought. If you have not had any children yet, now is the time to ask your partner:

- Do you feel ready to become a parent?
- Is there anything you want to do before becoming a parent?
- What excites you most about the idea of becoming a parent?
- What scares you most about the idea of becoming a parent?
- Are there any activities we do together as a couple that you absolutely do not want to give up after becoming a parent?
- Do you have any personal hobbies or commitments that you absolutely do not want to give up after becoming a parent?

- What aspects of a future baby or child's behaviour do you feel best equipped to deal with?
- What aspects of a future baby or child's behaviour do you feel least equipped to deal with?
- What message do you most want to pass on to your children?
- Do you feel ready to see me take on the role of a parent?
- Is there anything I could do that you would view as completely unacceptable?

When opening a dialogue, it is essential to ensure that you both want the same things before throwing yourselves into the new adventure that comes with having a child, or this happy event could deal a death blow to your relationship. Do not rush into things!

BABY SHOCK

Once your desire to start a family has become a reality and you have brought a child into the world, it can cause a certain degree of upheaval in your life. Your baby's arrival will shake up all of your usual habits and will profoundly change the course of your life. Furthermore, having a child can sometimes bring out the darker sides of the new parents' personalities. This phenomenon could be dubbed "baby shock".

"Baby shock" leads to the two parents separating after the birth of their child. In fact, many couples feel overwhelmed after their child is born and end up splitting up because they feel intimidated by the challenges ahead of them and are convinced that they will not be able to navigate them.

The causes of baby shock can be very diverse, and can arise as a result of problems or conflicts which you have not been able to address and which have manifested differently depending on each person's individual personality. These potential causes include failing to prepare appropriately before having a child, allowing yourself to be consumed by negative thoughts without discussing them with a trusted friend or family member or a professional counsellor, getting angry at your partner for one reason or another, or the mother being left exhausted by the pregnancy and birth and never getting the chance to recover. You may end up blaming each other for these problems, ignoring them or avoiding the subject.

This is why the importance of maintaining healthy, honest communication with your partner can never be overstated, and why you should not hesitate to make specific requests of them to ensure that they understand your needs. It may also be a good idea to talk to someone who has gone through a similar experience and ask them for advice. A good relationship is worth fighting for, especially when you have welcomed a new member of the family into the fold!

HELICOPTER PARENTING

"Helicopter parenting" is a relatively new concept which describes parents who meddle excessively in their child's life and are overprotective or overly demanding.

Some parents, especially mothers, would do anything for their children. They see this as pure selflessness, but it can actually stem from a kind of selfishness and possessiveness, and can leave the child feeling smothered as a result.

"Helicopter parents" generally impose very strict limits on their children, and will often go to incredible lengths to keep their children at home where they can keep an eye on them and make sure that nothing happens to them. This kind of attitude requires constant vigilance, and will lead to the child becoming incredibly dependent on the parent, who is prepared to do anything to ensure that the child never fails and never suffers any misfortune. This deprives the child of the life experience that they need in order to become an independent adult.

Children have the right to their privacy and their independence, and depriving them of these things will simply stir up anxiety within the family. In fact, when parents demand too much of their children, it puts everyone involved – parent and child alike – under enormous pressure to meet impossible standards, and maintaining the illusion of perfection on a daily basis is an exhausting charade. One potential outcome is that the child will become so terrified of disappointing their parents that they go to great lengths to avoid doing so, never daring to live life on their own terms.

If you think that you may have fallen into this trap, you should be proud of yourself for acknowledging the facts. With time, you will be able to identify some more specific situations in which you play the role of a helicopter parent. When these situations arise in the future, try to refrain from getting involved, unless your child is facing a genuine threat. Make sure that you have your priorities in order – after all, it is more important for your child to know to look both ways before crossing the road than to know that they should always wear their old shoes when playing in the garden.

At the very least, your child should be able to make mistakes, even though this will be a painful experience for everyone involved. If you do not give them the chance to learn from their errors, they will simply do as they are told without really understanding why, and they will be left incapable of making their own decisions or carving out a place for themselves in society. Do not get too involved when your children are filling out legal forms or deciding who to date – let them choose their own path. In fact, if you refrain from constantly bombarding them with unsolicited advice without giving them the chance to think for themselves, they will be more likely to ask for your opinion.

DOES HAVING CHILDREN KILL THE ROMANCE?

There are a lot of myths about how having children is the fastest way to suck the love out of a relationship. In fact, marriage itself often results in couples settling into a more mundane lifestyle filled with nothing but small talk, and having children will do nothing to remedy the situation because all your attention will be devoted to them. For those who already harbour doubts over whether or not they want children, this argument can be very off-putting.

Much is also made of the fact that babies can disturb their parents' sleep by crying during the night, while some people claim that men will no longer be attracted to a woman who has become a mother, and sometimes one parent has to take on the lion's share of domestic responsibilities while the other becomes less involved in their family life and throws themselves into their job or their hobbies instead. Furthermore, if the child is better behaved for one parent than for the other, it can stir up jealousy and resentment.

After having a child, some parents seem to entirely forget that they are their own person, and lose themselves in their new role. There are various explanations for this behaviour: some people are simply overwhelmed with love for their child, others imitate the behaviour they learned from their parents when they were children themselves, and still others are motivated by the desire to be perfect in their children's eyes.

Bear in mind that these are nothing more than stereotypes, and that you are the only one who can control your own fate. In practice, the more you fret over everyday problems, the more over-protective you will be of your children, which will lead you to divide your time more and more unequally. This will cause your relationship to deteriorate because of a lack of attention, and before you know it you will find yourself locked in a stifling routine. However, it is often the little things that will make the biggest difference and restore balance to your relationship.

It can be difficult to open up about your worries, but it is essential to take the time to breathe, look around, and realise that you are never the only one going through a particular situation. Try watching a film that tackles the subject in a humorous manner, as this will allow you to take a step back and laugh about these problems.

10 films to inspire you and lighten the mood
1. Life As We Know It
2. The Back-up Plan
3. Yours, Mine & Ours
4. Cheaper By The Dozen
5. I Don't Know How She Does It
6. Nine Months
7. What to Expect When You're Expecting
8. This Is 40
9. Knocked Up
10. Happiness Never Comes Alone

EMPTY NEST SYNDROME

As your child grows up, they will move more and more fully into their own world, and they will eventually fly the nest. Once they have built a life for themselves, your presence in their life will be much less constant.

When both parents have completely immersed themselves in their responsibilities towards their children, being forced to return to their original circumstances before they had children can come as a shock to the system, because it will feel as though they have forgotten how to interact with each other – in other words, the key component of their relationship was lost along the way.

It is a good idea to look ahead and prepare for this transition in the same way that you would prepare for retirement. It is crucial to let your children go – never try to keep them at home in an attempt to avoid being left alone with your partner again. You must recognise that this is an unavoidable step and accept that you will need some time to adjust to your new circumstances.

THE SECRETS TO A HEALTHY RELATIONSHIP

While neglecting your child and the well-rounded upbringing they deserve is, of course, out of the question, you should also avoid devoting 100% of your time to them and forgetting your partner, your dreams and everything that makes you who you are. Losing yourself in your new role as a parent can only lead to frustration.

There are also many couples whose attempts at keeping the spark alive are unsuccessful. This is often because they aim too high and decide to set aside an entire day – or more – for themselves as a romantic getaway. Of course, it is difficult to find this much time, and they end up giving up on their plans. However, you can always make small romantic gestures a part of your daily routine without too much effort, and you should never underestimate the intensity that brief moments of intimacy can have.

Once you get into certain habits, it can be difficult to get out of them, and we often fall into the trap of thinking that we need to make massive changes in order to solve a problem. In fact, it is often the smallest actions that make the biggest difference.

HOW MUCH IMPORTANCE ARE YOU PLACING ON YOUR RELATIONSHIP?

The test below will allow you to discover how much importance you place on your partner and your relationship with them in comparison to the other aspects of your family life. This will give you an idea of the exact nature of your situation and of the extent to which you need to restore balance within your family.

1. You are going on a family trip to the beach. You...

+ spend all of your time making sure that the children are safe

cuddle your partner while the children play beside you

° leave the children with another family so that you can go for a romantic stroll

2. Your partner is very stressed and irritable at the moment. You...

+ tell them to act more cheerfully for the kids' sake

ask the kids to play quietly so that your partner can rest

° suggest that you and your partner should go out to make them feel better

3. Your child surprises you in bed. You...

+ never let yourself get carried away like that again

wait a while and then go back to what you were doing

° talk to the children and then go back to what you were doing

4. Your neighbours start talking about how much their children wear them out. You...

+ reply that your kids are your greatest joy in life

tell them some of your own stories

° explain that your children give you some space from time to time

5. Your child is constantly trying to mono-polise your attention. You...

+ do as they ask as often as possible

lose your patience despite trying not to

° take some time to give them your full attention then go back to what you were doing

6. You notice that your partner is being overwhelmed by the youngest children. You...

+ have your own problems to deal with

give the children a few orders then go back to what you were doing

° see to one of the children, splitting the responsibilities 50/50

7. Your partner seems a bit down recently. You...

+ tell them to snap out of it

frequently ask them what is wrong

° have a long talk with them about it and try not to add to their worries

8. Your perfect day would involve...

+ making crafts and cooking with the children, then going for a walk as a family

playing with the children outside then cuddling up with your partner in the evening

° taking the children to visit their aunt and having a romantic afternoon with your partner

9. Your bedtime routine involves...

+ reading a story to the children, tucking them in, reading and falling asleep quickly

tucking the children in, watching TV as a couple then going to bed

° tucking the children in, doing something together as a couple, cuddling then going to bed

10. The thing that annoys you most about your partner is...

+ their indifference towards family matters

their tendency to go off and do things by themselves without asking you if you want to join them

° their overbearing attitude towards the children and the way they never listen to you

Plus: You devote very little time to your partner or none at all. Your home life revolves around your children, leaving very little time for you and your partner to spend together. You may even treat your partner like another one of your children and scold them if they do not pull their weight around the house or in the children's upbringing.

While it is important for your partner to consider the children a priority and to do their part, be careful that you do not boss them around to such an extent that they grow distant as a result. They may simply have a different approach to parenting, which is the reason why they do not seem to be giving you their full support. It may be a good idea to take a step back from your parental responsibilities and bring some fun back into your lives.

Hash: You devote some time to your partner. Although you are fully invested in your role as a parent, do everything you can to ensure that your children are safe and healthy and enjoy doing it, you and your partner also have a few little habits which let you keep your romance alive. You probably still find it difficult to keep everything under control, but you manage to take your partner's feelings into account and spend time together.

However, any time you start feeling overwhelmed, the time you spend together tends to dwindle until it simply involves watching TV together or stealing quick kisses in a corner. To spice things up, try to spend one evening a week doing something other than just watching TV, and make sure that you are taking your partner's desires into account.

Circle: You spend a great deal of time with your partner. You manage to split your time equally between your children and your partner, and your relationship with them is thriving. You still go on dates, have long conversations and spend time relaxing together. Of course, that does not mean that you neglect your children, but they probably have a bit more freedom, or help out around the house more than other children their age. Keep nurturing both

QUALITY TIME WITH YOUR CHILDREN

It is perfectly natural for a mother to spend almost all of her time with her newborn baby during the first few months after giving birth – after all, the past nine months will have been very intense for both mother and child. However, as time goes by it is essential to gradually return to a normal life and reduce the co-dependence between you and your child. Remember that your child does not actually need you to be hovering over them all the time, and that you can always ask a relative or close friend to look after them for a while, giving you some time that you can spend with your partner rekindling your passion for each other.

It is also essential to ensure that you are working with your partner to bring your children up properly. As time goes by, your goal should be to make sure that your child is gradually becoming capable of amusing themselves, is making friends that they can play with, etc. Naturally, you should pay attention to your child, especially by playing with them, but they should never feel like you are smothering them. Your goal should never be to spend all of your time with them, because this would be harmful not only to you, but also to your child and your relationship with your partner. In fact, while bonding with your child is incredibly fulfilling, you are likely to feel overwhelmed by their constant demands at a certain point, often to such an extent that you start dreaming of having some time to yourself. This is a clear sign that you both need to regain some independence so that your relationship with your child remains healthy.

The answer often lies in spending quality time with your child. Spend a limited amount of time with them, maybe around 25 minutes, giving them and the games you are playing together your undivided attention, and then return to your other responsibilities. This leaves your child feeling acknowledged and fulfilled, meaning that they will be more likely to give you some peace for a while. Remember that quality is often more important than quantity!

QUALITY TIME ALONE

Once you get into the habit of spending quality time with your children, you can start thinking about getting back in touch with your inner self through your goals and hobbies.

Since you will probably be fairly busy with both your professional and personal life, take small steps at first. Try reading a few pages of a novel, playing a piece of music, or starting a project which only requires five minutes of your time per day. As you get back into your old habits and your children grow up, you will be able to devote more time to these hobbies and get involved in more demanding activities.

If you give your partner the chance to take some time for themselves every now and then and are willing to take care of the children until they get back, they will be very grateful. Do not hesitate to ask them to return the favour so that one person is not always picking up the other's slack.

Remember that both of you need to be able to take some time to yourselves so that you can grow as individuals instead of spending all of your time stuck in your role as a parent.

QUALITY TIME WITH YOUR PARTNER

Once you get into the habit of making time to look after your own needs as well as spending quality time with your children, you should start focusing on your relationship with your partner.

Firstly, it is important to remember that you do not know everything about your partner. You do not know exactly what they are thinking or feeling at any given moment, and they will not always share those thoughts and feelings with you. Although a lot of their time is probably devoted to your child, deep down, your other half probably wishes that they could revitalise their relationship with you, although they may be unsure of how to do so.

Every individual and every relationship is unique, but everyone needs to spend at least some quality time with their partner and to receive a certain degree of attention from them, and you and your partner are no exception. It can be helpful to figure out what you and your partner's "love languages" are, meaning whether you prefer to express and receive affection through physical touch, gift giving, acts of service, quality time or words of affirmation. If you put your situation into perspective, you will see that it requires very little effort to bring a spark of joy into your partner's life a few times every week.

After all, it is a small matter to take a few seconds to give your partner a kiss when your child calls you to come and play with them. Or why not kill two birds with one stone by buying something special for your partner while you are looking for a little gift for your child? If you are prepared to go to the effort of planning a trip for your child and their friends down to the very last details, surely your partner deserves a similar amount of attention? After all, there are two days in the weekend, meaning that you have enough time to divide your attentions equally.

Finally, if your partner likes to hear you express your love for them or appreciates you regularly lending them a helping hand, you will have many chances to show them how much you care every single week. Your goal should not be to make a single sweeping declaration of love, but to make it obvious through little everyday gestures.

QUALITY OVER QUANTITY

Quality time can be as brief as five stolen minutes or as long as an entire day. It is up to you to figure out how long you need depending on what you want and what kind of activities you are going to do. This is a time when you should be focusing all of your attention on your loved one (or on yourself).

During the quality time you spend with your partner, you will be fully immersed in an activity that you have both agreed on, whether that is having a drink, telling them about your day, having a cuddle, playing a board game, visiting an exhibition – the list is endless! The important thing is that both of you enjoy the activity and that it is a source of good memories.

Your aim should be to take some time to recharge your batteries without any interruptions, so you should try to get rid of any distractions, like your phones and the internet. In other words, you should take some time to distance yourselves from the rest of the world and spend a few moments living life to the full, away from external distractions.

Bear in mind that your children will grow up and leave home someday, leaving you and your partner to your own devices. As such, it is worth investing in your relationship ahead of time.

> "We still spend time together as a couple. In the evenings, we have a tipple and a nice meal, then cuddle up together to watch TV. Our families are supportive, and sometimes take care of our son for a while. We also like to exchange "sweet nothings", like sharing a quick kiss when we walk past each other down the hall, or leaving a little note in the other's gym bag – little things like that." (Lucy, 29)

ASKING FOR HELP WHEN YOU NEED IT

Sometimes, one partner seems to take far less of an interest in their children's upbringing than the other. This generally leads to the partner who puts in more effort feeling abandoned and resentful because of the unfairness of the situation, and they will probably struggle to conceal these emotions. Why might your other half fail to offer you enough help, even though they should be your main source of strength?

It goes without saying that you should never assume that you know exactly what your partner is feeling. Consider the idea that they may be struggling to find their place within the family. If you never ask them to lend a hand, they may get the impression that you are perfectly capable of handling everything by yourself and start feeling useless. Although no one likes admitting that they need help, you will probably be surprised by how much your partner is willing to do for you if you ask. They will also appreciate the chance to play a larger role in contributing to your children's wellbeing and your personal wellbeing.

However, your partner may feel stressed out because of external factors, and feeling pressure at home to be a perfect parent can exacerbate this stress. The fear of being a bad parent can be crippling, and can affect anyone. Always be there to listen if they need to talk about the things that are bothering them. If you are struggling to find a quick solution for a deep-rooted problem, spending some time talking about it can make all the difference. No matter what difficulties you face, never forget to communicate with your partner, as you will be surprised by just how much weight a good conversation can take off your shoulders.

CHILDCARE AND BABYSITTING

By making gradual adjustments to your lifestyle, your relationship will gradually find its feet again. Make sure that you set aside some longer periods of time to spend together as well as sharing smaller romantic gestures. While it is important to spend time together as a family and to introduce your children to a variety of activities, you also have the right to live a full, fulfilling life as an adult.

The first step is to figure out whether you want

a quiet night at home or if you would prefer to go out for an evening or a weekend. Would you rather spend an evening playing video games, playing board games, or exploring the city? Once you make your decision, try to stick to it instead of giving up at the first hurdle (you are too busy, one of the children has a cold, bad weather, etc.), or you may end up never putting your plans into action.

> "Having a lie-in becomes a thing of the past when you have kids. However, you can still go out and keep up your hobbies if you are willing to make the effort to stay organised. You can even keep going on holiday, whether alone, as a couple, or as a family." (Paul, 41)

The second step is to make a list of people whom you trust to look after your children from time to time. This list can include friends, relatives and babysitters, and should ideally include a variety of people so that you do not always have to leave your children with the same people.

If you tend to worry a lot, try to gradually create some breathing distance between you and your child. Learn to trust other people and try to avoid calling them every single time you feel worried. Bear in mind that spending time with other people is a learning experience for your child, which will open their mind and give them the opportunity to try new things. When they come home, they will have lots of things to tell you.

<u>**EVERYDAY WORK**</u>

There are many different ways of nourishing your relationships with your partner, your children and with yourself.

- **With yourself**
  - Think about how you view your relationship and how you approach your children's upbringing.
  - Ask for help and delegate where necessary.
  - Ask your partner to look after the children.
  - Give yourself time to read, to take care of yourself by doing sport, etc.
  - Take a step back from challenging situations and speak up about them.
  - Clearly state what you want and look for practical, creative solutions.

- **With your partner**
  - Take time to communicate when something is wrong.
  - Do not deprive yourselves of physical contact; for example, curl up together to watch TV in the evenings.
  - Leave sweet little messages around the house for each other on sticky notes.
  - Buy a little surprise (a book, an ornament, chocolate, etc.) for your partner.
  - Give them compliments.
  - Spend quality time together: board games, museum visits, cinema, walks, ballroom dancing or cooking classes, etc.
  - Look after the children while your partner is busy.

- **With your children**
  - Give them your undivided attention for a brief, specific length of time.
  - Play a game together.
  - Read them a story.
  - Tell them the story of how you fell in love with your partner.
  - Pick a babysitter that everyone likes.

TEACH YOUR CHILDREN TO RESPECT YOUR PRIVACY

You and your partner have the right to enjoy some privacy away from your children. One way of making this a reality is to tell the children to stay in one part of the house for a certain period of time while you and your partner retreat to a different part of the house. Good communication is essential – make sure that your children realise that this time is important for both of you, and that they need to respect it.

Do not be discouraged if they object to this plan, perhaps because they are used to being able to monopolise your attention. Of course, remind them that they can interrupt your private time if they encounter a real, serious problem (and not just that they have spilled something on their shirt or that their sibling just ate the last packet of crisps). This approach teaches children not to encroach on their parents' private life and to respect their need for privacy. Do not forget that if you have already spent some quality time with your child, they will be more willing to leave you in peace. Once they feel safe and cared for, there will be nothing stopping you from spending some time with your partner alone in your bedroom.

It is also perfectly acceptable to close doors to set some boundaries. If your family is very close and tends to spend a lot of time together in the living room, you can still escape occasionally and be sociable some other time.

So what is your current situation like? If finding the time for these little moments of privacy seems impossible, try filling out the questionnaire below to pinpoint the problem. You will soon see that it is entirely possible to take practical action to improve a situation that is causing problems. Pay attention to the reasons why you cannot seem to escape from your children, as some of these reasons have deeper roots than others, and you may need to talk to your partner or with a psychologist in order to resolve the issue.

PUT YOURSELF TO THE TEST

How important is the role your children play in your life?

- When does it feel as though your children

are interfering with your romantic relationship?
- Have you ever tried to change the situation?   Yes/No
- If not, why?
  ◦ my children would not listen to me;
  ◦ it is difficult to break old habits;
  ◦ I have no right to want time to myself;
  ◦ I have never really thought about it;
  ◦ I value the time I spend with my children
    more than time to myself or the time I
    spend with my partner;
  ◦ other.

- If you have, what approach did you take
  and why do you think it failed?
- What immediate steps could you take
  in order to improve your relationship?
  Do you have any ideas, big or small? Do
  not hesitate to put them into practice,
  because trying out a variety of strategies
  will help you to make gradual changes.
  Even the smallest gestures can make a
  difference.

EVERYDAY DISPLAYS OF AFFECTION

Some couples feel embarrassed at the thought of kissing in front of their children. They think that it is "not done" or feel uncomfortable at the thought of having an innocent onlooker while they embrace, and so all physical affection is confined to the bedroom. However, displays of affection serve to remind your children that you love each other, and children who never see their parents embracing often begin to assume that they do not love each other anymore. Some children may even feel guilty, imagining that they have done something wrong and that it is their fault that their parents do not love each other anymore.

Public displays of affection are a way of showing your child that love and long-term relationships are very real. By staying in the habit of giving your partner a quick kiss or cuddle when the mood strikes, you will also ensure that the strength of your loving relationship with them does not wane. Of course, you are the only ones who can decide what is right for your relationship, and the most important thing is for both partners to feel comfortable and secure together. If you are not a particularly tactile pair, you will probably not feel the need to snuggle up together very often. On the other hand, if you both like to show how much you care, it is important not to deprive yourself of the physical contact you crave.

If one of you is quite tactile while the other is more reserved, try to find some compromises so that you can both feel comfortable. Never force yourself to do something which makes you feel uncomfortable – there are a whole host of different approaches you can take, from a simple peck on the cheek to more intimate embraces, and you will always be able to find something that you are both comfortable with. Take the time to explore the different possibilities together and figure out what you both enjoy most.

When it comes to your sex life, many couples have a hard time dealing with the drop in libido that often accompanies a new addition to the family. Simply getting a good night's sleep when there is a baby in the next room can sometimes feel like an elaborate obstacle course, which leads to romance falling prey to exhaustion, and sometimes when a new mother is running herself ragged to look after the newborn, the father still manages to feel indignant that he no longer commands her full attention. However, having a child can actually enhance your sex life, so long as you can accept the fact that things will never be exactly the same. Savour the intimate moments you share, and focus on the simple pleasure of having them instead of on their length or how frequent they are. Simple touches, showing that you care for each other, taking a bath together and so on are just some of the ways you can keep your sex life healthy and active.

BIG SOLUTIONS FOR BIG PROBLEMS

If small gestures are not enough to restore balance to your relationship, think back over your personal history. You could do so through psychotherapy or Family Constellations sessions, for example.

Family Constellations is a method of exploring your family history through regular individual or group sessions, or in stages. This is a form of therapy which allows you to gain a better understanding of certain problematic behaviours you may exhibit and the factors which prevent you from fully embracing who you are. During each session, someone plays the role of one of your family members, which helps you to confront reality head-on and sheds some light on the problems you have faced and the coping mechanisms you have adopted to deal with them. These coping mechanisms are often no longer needed and may have become a burden and a hindrance over time.

Family and couples therapy are also powerful tools which can help you to understand and manage the mental blocks and defence mechanisms that could be undermining your relationships with your partner and your family. In order for this therapy to be effective, you will need to talk to your other half and to your children about taking this step and make sure that they know how important it is for both you personally and for the family as a whole. Of course, you should choose the type of therapy that seems best suited to you and your situation, but you should also make your decision based on whether or not you would be able to persevere with it in the long run. It is very important to feel comfortable in these kinds of situations.

Nonetheless, there are a few simple tips you can follow on a daily basis to help keep your relationship healthy, and they may well be enough to keep your relationship on the right track without seeking professional help. In the table below we have also outlined ten pitfalls to avoid – but remember that these are only guidelines, and every couple is different. If something works for you, embrace it!

10 pitfalls to avoid	10 strategies to follow
1. Calling your partner "mum" or "dad", as you run the risk of forgetting that they are first and foremost your partner and forcing them to take on a larger role than they are prepared for.	1. Establish little rituals for you and your partner.
2. Never talking about anything other than the children.	2. Remain confident in your sexuality.
3. Letting the children sleep in your bed.	3. Take naps with your partner if you are having trouble getting enough sleep at night.
4. Letting yourself go and not taking care of yourself.	4. Talk to each other and take up common hobbies, even if you cannot devote much time to them.
5. Letting problems build up over time.	5. Plan your outings in advance so that you know you will soon have some time to yourselves, which will help you to relax.

10 pitfalls to avoid	10 strategies to follow
6. Focusing all of your attention on your child and neglecting your partner.	6. Take advantage of any time your child spends sleeping or playing by themselves.
7. Never denying any of your child's requests.	7. Make a list of possible babysitters so that you have the chance to go out with your partner from time to time.
8. Trying to handle everything alone.	
9. Letting toys get scattered all around the house, which will make it feel as though your room belongs to the children instead of you.	8. Do not be too hard on yourself – no parent is perfect!
	9. Communicate with your partner as much as possible.
10. Making fun of your partner's mistakes in front of their family, their friends or your children.	10. Find a way to unwind as soon as you start feeling overwhelmed.

The important thing is to find the right balance by following these guidelines and figuring out what works for your relationship. Above all, do not forget that having a child should never spell the end of your love life – it is simply the beginning of a new chapter!

FAQS

OUR CHILD DOES NOT WANT TO LET US HAVE ANY TIME TO OURSELVES. WHAT SHOULD WE DO?

Ask yourself if you might be partially responsible for letting your child interfere in your relationship with your partner. This does not mean that you should blame yourself, but it is important to understand what caused this situation. It is normal to have moments of weakness when spending time with your family, but this does not mean that there is no way to remedy the situation.

In order to make more time for your relationship, you must begin by making it clear that it is an important part of your family dynamics. You need to highlight the fact that in addition to being parents, you are also individuals with your own lives and passions and a loving couple with shared interests.

Gradually establish some habits which help your child to realise that you are busy and that they will have to entertain themselves for a while. The goal is not to hold them permanently at arm's length, but to make sure that everything has its own time and place, which means that while you can play with the children at times, they will also have to play by themselves sometimes while you are otherwise occupied or spending time with your partner.

Bear in mind that these changes do not happen overnight, and a certain amount of communication will be necessary in order to find a compromise that suits everyone. However, this process is worth the effort because it will breathe new life into your romantic relationship while also giving your child more independence and teaching them not to rely on you as much.

SHOULD WE BE THINKING ABOUT HAVING A SECOND CHILD EVEN IF WE HAD DIFFICULTY ADJUSTING WHEN WE HAD OUR FIRST CHILD?

Just because your first experience of parenthood was not exactly plain sailing, it does not mean that you should avoid having more children.

However, it is wise to put a lot of thought into the decision, as this will help you to avoid making the same mistakes as before.

First of all, have a long conversation with your partner to try and identify the main problems you encountered when you had your first child and the reasons why you want to have another baby. Make sure that you are both ready to become a parent for the second time, taking all of your personal plans, limits and past events into account.

If your main reason for wanting to have another child is because you want to fix everything that went wrong the first time, it is definitely not a good idea. You would be better off reflecting on how you could improve your current family situation so that every member of the family feels acknowledged, secure and content.

In any case, if you had difficulties when your first child was born, this does not necessarily mean that it will be equally difficult the second time around. Communication is crucial – you need to find the courage to say whatever is on your mind, to ask other parents or a psychologist for any help you need and to dismiss the idea of having a second child, whether temporarily or permanently, if you do not feel ready.

WHAT ASPECTS OF BECOMING A PARENT CAN THREATEN A ROMANTIC RELATIONSHIP?

The main threat to your romantic relationship after you have children is the temptation to start constantly focusing all of your attention on your offspring. This can lead you to neglect both your inner life and your romantic relationship, and private moments between you and your partner will become a thing of the past, even around the home.

Instead of asking your partner about their day, cheering them up and distracting them, you will start concentrating solely on your children's successes and failures, the back-to-school supplies you need to buy and your worries about their education. You will then start to forget about your personal needs and the needs of your relationship, which can have serious consequences.

WHAT SPECIFIC STEPS CAN WE TAKE TO GET OUR CHILDREN TO RESPECT OUR NEED FOR PRIVACY?

In order to get your children to respect your need for privacy, you should set aside certain periods of time and let your children know that you are not to be disturbed during that time. Use simple terms to explain to them that you want to spend some time alone together as a couple.

You should also make it clear that certain rooms will be off-limits to them during this time, and if you are worried that your children may not respect your need for privacy and might barge into the room you are in, do not hesitate to lock the door. You should also teach your children to knock before entering while they are still very young. However, you should remind them that you will always be available if they really need you.

WHEN IS IT APPROPRIATE TO LEAVE PARENTAL RESPONSIBILITIES TEMPORARILY ASIDE?

Although you are now full-time parents, this does not mean that you need to be a constant presence in your children's lives. Even though the media and some people you know will make you feel as though you should be doing more for your children and doing everything better, remember that every family is different and that perfectionism is a toxic attitude.

Get into the habit of making the most of the moments when your child is entertaining themselves alone in their room, playing with their siblings in the playroom or staying with a different family member or with friends. Although it may not be easy, have some faith in your children and in the people who are looking after them. Once you have taught them all the most important safety rules, they will be able to identify and avoid danger by themselves, whereas constantly hovering over them prevents them from having enriching life experiences and developing their independence.

Being a doting parent who keeps an eye on their children is very different to constantly meddling in their lives at the slightest provocation, or before they even get into difficulties. If you give them more freedom, they will be more inclined to come to you when they do have a problem. It can also be a good idea to ask your friends and family to keep an eye on your children as well and to warn you if they are in any real danger.

WHAT CAN WE DO TO FORESTALL CRITICISM FROM THOSE AROUND US REGARDING OUR PARENTING METHODS?

There will always be people who have a tendency to preach at you about the way they think you should be raising your children, or who like to stick their nose where it does not belong. Even if they have good intentions, over time they can make you feel guilty about taking a different approach. However, it is very difficult to change other people's behaviour. Try to listen carefully and sift through what they say, taking any good advice on board while ignoring the bad advice.

If you believe that your family is thriving, there is no reason to change your approach simply because other people do things differently. Pressure from the media or from the people around you can often stir up doubts which are unproductive and do nothing but make you miserable. You do not owe anyone else an explanation – just because other parents are very overprotective, it does not mean that you should copy them. Even though some trends are becoming more and more common in our society, such as helicopter parenting, everything depends on context and our individual hopes and dreams. Every family is different!

HOW CAN WE JUGGLE OUR PROFESSIONAL, FAMILY AND ROMANTIC LIVES SIMULTANEOUSLY?

Managing your time effectively is no easy task. Stay-at-home parents often feel as though they are living in a constant war zone which leaves them unable to take any time for themselves, while parents who work away from home often wish that they could spend more time with their children.

Both of these situations can lead you to sacrifice your romantic relationship so that you can give your children as much attention as possible. If this is the case for you, take an objective view of the situation and try to identify any particularly time-consuming habits or attitudes, such as constantly supervising your children while they are playing, and replace them with quality time spent with your partner. Even fleeting moments are precious and are always better than nothing!

HOW CAN I MAKE MY PARTNER REALISE THAT THEY ARE SPENDING TOO MUCH TIME WITH THE CHILDREN?

If you feel like your partner is focusing too much of their attention on your children, it can quickly become a nagging concern. You should be open with them about how you are feeling and try to find a solution, as they may not realise that they have been giving you the cold shoulder.

Take your partner aside and make sure that

you have their full attention when explaining your feelings to them so that you can be sure that they have fully understood the problem. Try to use neutral language by focusing on your perspective and feelings instead of criticising their behaviour: for example, instead of saying something accusatory like "you spend too much time with the children", try saying "I feel like our relationship has been on stand-by since we had the kids" or "I've been feeling left out since we became parents". Be clear and direct, explaining exactly how you would like to change your daily life and routine.

Suggest some potential solutions that would suit both of you. It is unfair to expect your partner to make sudden, drastic changes, so opt for clear goals that you can work towards gradually, and remember to acknowledge their efforts and let them know that you appreciate them.

We want to hear from you!
Leave a comment on your online library
and share your favourite books on social media!

FURTHER READING

BIBLIOGRAPHY

- Bodenmann, G. (2003) *Une vie de couple heureuse.* Paris: Odile Jacob.

- Devienne, E. (2007) *Être femme sans être mère. Le choix de ne pas avoir d'enfant.* Paris: Robert Laffont.

- Fernandez, Y. (2005) *Proverbes psy pour mieux vivre.* Paris: Eyrolles.

- Gordon, T. (2008) *Parent Effectiveness Training: The Proven Program for Raising Responsible Children.* Three Rivers Press: California.

- Nemet-Pier, L. (2015) *Aimer ses enfants sans se laisser dévorer.* Paris: Albin Michel.

- Pellé Douel, C. (2015) Les enfants détruisent-ils la vie intime ? *Psychologies.com.* [Online]. [Accessed 24 November 2017]. Available from: <http://www.psychologies.com/Couple/Vie-de-couple/Au-quotidien/Articles-et-Dossiers/Reussir-sa-vie-de-couple/Les-enfants-detruisent-ils-la-vie-intime>

- Purves, L. (1994) *Comment ne pas être une famille parfaite.* Paris: Pocket.

- Quenneville, D. (2014) Comment le couple peut surmonter le "baby clash ? *Laligue.be.* [Online]. [Accessed 24 November 2017]. Available from: <https://www.laligue.be/leligueur/articles/comment-le-couple-peut-surmonter-le-baby-clash>

- Salomé, J. (2009) Enfermée dans votre rôle de mère. *Psychologies.com.* [Online]. [Accessed 24 November 2017]. Available from: <http://www.psychologies.com/Famille/Etre-parent/Mere/Articles-et-Dossiers/Enfermee-dans-votre-role-de-mere>

- Vaineau, A. (2016) 5 conseils pour éviter le babyclash. *Psychologies.com.* [Online]. [Accessed 24 November 2017]. Available from: <http://www.psychologies.com/Famille/Etre-parent/Equilibre-du-couple/Articles-et-Dossiers/5-conseils-pour-eviter-le-baby-clash/4Parvenir-a-faire-equipe>